ALSO BY JEAN O'BRIEN

Working the Flow
(Lapwing Chapbook, 1992)

The Shadow Keeper
(Salmon, 1997)

Reach
(Lapwing Chapbook, 2004)

Dangerous Dresses
(Bradshaw Books, 2005)

Lovely Legs
(Salmon, 2009)

Merman
(Salmon, 2012)

salmonpoetry

*Celebrating 35 Years
of Literary Publishing*

Fish On A Bicycle
New & Selected Poems

Jean O'Brien

Published in 2016 by
Salmon Poetry
Cliffs of Moher, County Clare, Ireland
Website: www.salmonpoetry.com
Email: info@salmonpoetry.com

ISBN 978-1-910669-58-7

COVER IMAGE: *Kevin McSherry – www.mcsherry.ie*
COVER DESIGN & BOOK TYPESETTING: *Siobhán Hutson*
Printed in Ireland by Sprint Print

Salmon Poetry gratefully acknowledges the support of
The Arts Council / An Chomhairle Ealaóin

For my lifelong friend
Bernard Downes (1949-2013)
Thank you for the days.

Acknowledgements

As well as previously uncollected poems, *Fish on a Bicycle — New & Selected Poems* includes work from the following collections: *Working the Flow* (Lapwing Chapbook, 1992), *The Shadow Keeper* (Salmon, 1997), *Reach* (Lapwing Chapbook, 2004), *Dangerous Dresses* (Bradshaw Books, 2005) *Lovely Legs* (Salmon, 2009) and *Merman* (Salmon, 2012).

For first publications of poems in this book, grateful acknowledgement is made to the editors of the following: Arvon International Poetry Prize (Winner), *Agenda* (UK), *Between the Circus and the Sewer*, Chapman (UK), *Cloverdale Anthology* (ed. Patrick Cotter as part of the Cloverdale Prize), *Cyphers*, Fish International Poetry Prize (winner), *Fortnight Magazine*, Forward Prize (Highly Commended), Gregory O'Donoghue Prize (Commended), New *Hibernia Review* (Featured Poet) (USA), *Icarus* TCD, *Interim* (USA), *The Irish Times*, *Trinity Broadsheet, Prairie Schooner* (USA), *Stony Thursday*, *Tandem* (UK), *The SHOp*, *Visions* (USA). Some of the poems were broadcast on RTÉ's *The Arts Show*, *The Darkness Echoing* and *Sunday Miscellany*.

Special thanks to Kevin McSherry, artist, illustrator and friend, for the kind use of his print for my cover.

Contents

from DANGEROUS DRESSES (2005)

from LOVELY LEGS (2009)

from MERMAN (2012)

NEW POEMS (2012-2015)

from
Working The Flow
(1992)

The Dreaming

In my Dreamtime I was the lizard,
skin smooth, yet scaled
the contradictions of the Chameleon
without the colour,
for I had the colour of the rock
grey, green warm and dry as the sand.
My dance was the dance
of perfect stillness.
Reposed amongst the rocks
only my darting tongue
would betray my presence.
In the dry hot wind
the smell of raw loneliness
coming off me was like a skin
that could not form.
The desert sun is too harsh,
the hot sand like pumice
strips off the grace notes
while my skin shifts to encompass
the loss.

The Charnel House

Twentieth century wisdom makes us scoff
at people who once thought the world was flat,
perhaps it was for them;
stretching out arid and bare
and weighting on the heart like a stone
lodged in the ribcage,
chaffing on bone.
The Charnel House is filled with such things,
heaped together on the ashen floor.
Now in Turin they tell us
that the Lord bore nails in his ankles
rather than his feet.
A nail crushing bone is still a nail,
whether it is smashing through
thick ankle joints or the delicate
filigree in our feet.

In a Stout Jar

Quiet now the night, that long
drawn out sigh,
an hour now stands between me
and soft daylight.
A short reprieve, one dusky hour
to armour myself,
against the day's effacing bustle.
Quickly I run to store
the night's impossible wantings,
in a stout jar, high on
some dusty shelf.

Samhain *(November's Eve)*

Climb into my bed he urged me
with a voice all sweet reason,
the light from the moon shimmering
in his dark eyes as he held me.
With morning the sun sliced the patterns
of the wall stones and I slitted my eyes
to make things splinter and to make
sparks fly.

I kept the hoard hidden,
glinting under the bed
the weighty silver chalice
all a-sparkle with its studs
of glass and amber.
Stolen.
Stolen for you child, conceived
on this feast of all souls unsettled,
on sheets smooth as the island
and the bog surrounding it
black and sodden.

No better place to hide the treasure.
I'll go there at dusk
when the darkness and rustle of wind
will smother my movements.
Tied tight in the sack
with the chalice
I'll bury the amulet,
with the gold fibulas and bronze spoons —
They want the treasure sprung from my womb
but for that, I'll want prizes.

They'll think twice now in Derrynaflan
before asking a good woman like me
to bed down with a priest
for all that he be a man,
and twice again when they
count up the days and dates
and seasons
and realise that last night
was November's Eve.

Celebrating the Light of the Moon

Rita Ann asked, was it the moon
that brought her to the maternity;
and glad I was to hear her answer.
I had thought it was the 14A bus;
reared on stories of frantic journeys
at midnight, petrol running low
and the woman with not long to go,
pleading 'hurry, please hurry'.
Me constantly asking 'but how will
I know?' Brusque answers, 'Oh you will
know when the time is right'.
Me knowing damn well I wouldn't
and didn't.
The designated date long past,
at last bored I picked up my case
and boarded the 14A bus.
So glad I was for Rita Ann
that she had a bit of excitement,
all I saw was the low tide of the Liffey
as I paid the conductor, one fare
with defiance. Damned if I'd pay
a double yet, it still being daylight
and me on my own.

Staying with the Nuns

It was all so familiar and different,
outside the noise, bells ringing,
the constant jangle of 8th Avenue
woke me from sleep.

When I opened my eyes
they met the brown stained
door, the high polish of an old
linoleum floor, dull convent paint
on the walls. Ireland in New York.

Back with the nuns after twenty
five years, the old fear flashed
bridging the time in a second,
as I found myself smiling
appeasement at the sisters.

Tiptoeing across the floor afraid
of discovery for a crime I never
quite put my finger on, am sure
I never committed, or was the crime
the just being there?

Everest

On our way up, we pass used gas cylinders,
aquamarine water bottles, yellow high-vis tents,
torn and useless, old socks, a boot still spiked.
Rags of what were clothes are banner strips
lashed by wind, a constant flutter.
it's all still there on the mountain.

Suddenly we see her, sitting in low sunlight,
in this vast desert of snow.
Her fair hair waving in the Himalayan breeze.
We smile, shout a greeting, think
we recognise her. The Sherpas hurry us
upwards, tug at our guide ropes, sink their axes
in the snow, jam their crampons in.

They pull us up the ladders at Khumbu Icefall,
a web of rope entwines us, they call back
through flaying wind. She is a grave-less
ghost. In summer sun melts the permafrost,
ice falls away, she is revealed, sitting
where she stopped, rooted there. Her face
drying to a leather tan, her hair bleached

by years of sun. In her frozen garden
the elements are slowly undressing her,
she is being stripped off as the mountain
sculpts itself around her, folding her in.
We are heading for the Hillary steps,
crevasses yawn before us. Then, as if reaching
for the heavens, we climb on.

Learning Death

Star fingers flutter in alarm
and poke at the black thing
that doesn't stir.
A wound oozes blood and the mother
fearful of germs
pulls at the child.
'Mammy, Mammy it won't fly'.
She cries while her mother
tell her death;
the silent – still – black – nothingness.
The no more of it.
She learns death in flowers and flies
and the goldfish she thought
was just swimming upside down
his golden silvery sheen
whiting out.

Years later as she sat all night
beside the still and waxy figure.
she wondered if her mother
had been teaching her
her own death.
Her mother's limbs disentangled now
from the clawing at her life.
Her eyes not quite closed
as if at any moment
they might flutter open.
Her hands folded into peaceful
fingers might just reach up
and chase away the fly
that landed on her temple.

Oh there were things about
that long might,
she felt she should protect
her mother from.

from
The Shadow Keeper
(1997)

Black Sheets

Black sheets on my warm bed.
Sometimes I share them with my silky cat.
Black on Black. Only her green eyes show.
My son is in safe harbour here,
his thin pink limbs
etched to an outline.

Lovers come to me, some joyous, some
in deceit. Our bodies lie together.
We weave our words and limbs and make
a different story.
Tell it to ourselves so often
it lodges in our history.
Plump feathers cradle us
and we go back
to where we live without
world things.

Body Talk

My fingers seek you
as words search the tongue
for utterance. Your skin
a wordless flow under my hand,
friction of silk as skin on skin
makes quiet conversation
with cool linen.
I feast on your sleeping face,
you pleasure my eye.
Freeze the moment, make it stay
simple as that.
Later we will rise, dress in armour,
embrace in challenge to fence
with spiked words while last night's
fingerprints vanish
on our skin.

Wheeling Down the Towpath

Nearly everyday of my life
I observed you. I remember
as a child playing by the river,
when your old black bike wheeled down
the towpath and my sudden
urgency to keep up with you –
Although on child's legs I ran and ran,
I fell further and further behind.

Your puzzled surprise when later
I stumbled through the door
out of breath and crying; the image
of your receding shape is locked
in my mind. Now your are receding
again. As you fall further and further
into age, your small fussings irritate me,
the ceremony of your narrowing days
wheeling down like your old black bike,
as you fill the time you are marking.

Stumbling towards a future which,
like the long ago towpath,
simply ran out of river.
I wait now for the sign
that will tell me to stop following
and finally let you go.

Winter Resolved

All winter I walked the river bank,
searching for the familiar
grey of the heron.
I had watched him through two
summers and winters.

All winter I was caught between
the calls of my new child and my dying
father, stretched to my limits,
trapped midway between the pull
of youth and age as they seemed
to sound each other out through
the sleepless nights, both struggling
to keep their foothold.

As my daughter's coos and cries
grew louder, my father's frets and murmurs
quietened. I heard her
drowning him out.

Now with the first hints of spring,
I find my heron. He stands stock still
on his high legs above the waterfall.
No quiver betraying his effort
to keep balance.

Drowning at Sherkin

i.m. Pat Moran

Clothes folded neatly
by the edge of the lake, shoes
weighting them down; edging out
from under his sketch pad,
a pencilled outline waiting to be filled.
His watch hidden inside a sock,
marks his time as he entered
the lake water, slate grey and smooth
with trouble underneath.

I stood in the Gallery before Yeats' *Grief*
and saw him there, centred in the lake
astride a white horse, a towering
rampart beside. The picture all edged
yellow for spite, deep blue for regret
and red for rage as he floundered
in the water, drowned in a tissue of colours
just clear of the Cape.

First Sins

Tucked into a large bed
that filled up most of the box room,
my sister and I off school
with scarlet fever.
Ravenous with rash and raw throats,
we rifled granny's bag
and found a cornucopia, to a fifties child –
round orange suns, a whole fat bag of them –
mother downstairs, tired from the fetch
and carry of two cantankerous children.

We hesitated, held one magnificent
orange orb aloft, admired
its perfect roundness,
listened carefully for footfall
on the stairs, and then with flinty nails
made the first break, the juice
a balm on our aching throats.
Having committed the first sin,
in a mess of pith and rind
we ate the lot.

A Stout Tree

Raggedy Ann went down the street
with a whistle, a pair of blue shorts
and a rope. She was twelve years old.
Her mother told her it was impolite
to whistle, tomboyish to wear shorts
and dangerous to play with ropes.

Raggedy Ann was content, those three sins
had cheered her up no end. Besides
she had heard her mother whistle
when she thought she was alone and bet
she'd much prefer to wear trousers
if she could get away with it.
So that left only the rope.

Raggedy tied the rope to a stout tree
twice around and then tied herself to it.
She looked odd, this girl who had tied
herself to a tree. A boy passing
inquired what she was doing.
I'm practicing, she said, *Practicing
to be myself.*

The Recipe

Every Christmas I take out her old book,
its leaves browned, the paper
dried to tissue. Carefully I turn the pages
and smile at recipes for invalids –
beef tea, real lemonade –
until I get to the cakes
where her hand jotted on the margins
her own preferred mix of raisins, sultanas,
orange peel and cherries, The ink
vanishes into the crumbling edge.

I still have her baking tin
greased up to hold off the rust.
I weigh and sift her every word
looking for some meaning
in the method. All I find are weights
and measures all doled out in pounds
and ounces the only recipe
I ever took from her.
I am uneasy till it rises.

Her Old Black Bike

If I shut my eyes very tight
I can recreate the bike,
your old black bone-shaker,
its basket hung up front,
the paint long dulled and lusterless
the pedals hanging rust-encrusted,
a wire back-carrier tied with twine.

If I concentrate even harder,
I can see you mount it
shedding years as you push
the pedals, wind streaming
past your ears, your hair loosed,
your skirt a banner unfurled.

When you were firmly earthbound
again and not watching,
I used to sneak a ride,
wanting to transform myself,
to push against the wind and through it,
ringing the bell loudly all the while.

All That Jazz

Why did you go there, I asked her,
what for? She looked at me as if
I were stupid. *You know* –
but I didn't, couldn't understand
the look of hurt in her grey eyes.
I remember seeing them like that
before, when she was a child
and going past our gate had noticed
an arm pointing to the sky,
protruding from under the lid
of the bin. She gave it a yank,
it was Raggedy Anne, she rescued her,
desperately trying to brush
the dirt of potato peel and tea leaves
from Raggedy's round moon face.
Her eyes had that same faraway
hurt look then as now.
Again I tried, *But Why?* She looked
at me with a shrug, *For love*, she said,
her face taking on like the moon,
For love and all that Jazz.

Census

A census taken in 1837 in an area of Donegal with 9,000
inhabitants found that they possessed in total 10 beds.

Stones like steps on the road,
heavy, hard and hungry.
The hedges stripped of haws and berries,
fields once full of yellow dandelions,
hung ears of corn and swaying wheat,
all bare like my children
standing in their shifts,
their petticoats
bartered for corn bread.

Before us the road goes nowhere.
Behind, the cottage is tumbled,
bedding itself down into the hard acres.
I have no furniture to speak of,
just one copper pot given
on marriage by my mother
tied now with twine about my waist,
echoing like a bell in empty space.

Threading Down Deep

The light leaches from the sky
to the lake, the unruffled surface
mirrored back its peaty depth,
the trees at our feet
felled and shorn, curlicues of bark
softened our footfall.

Near the waterfall we climb
over stones, hand over hand
you help me over,
and point out boulders
streaked chalky white.
We talk of famine roads
going nowhere and back.

We have been guilty of naming things,
mapping them out on the track,
pinning them down
like dressmakers' patterns
and always cutting
on the bias.

from
Reach
(2004)

Blind Russians Visit Dublin

They came to visit us, the poets, with their wares,
cameras, telescopes, binoculars all related to the eye.
By their sightless gaze we saw they could not see the light,
the gleam of shade and shadow, they lived by touch and echoes.
Their guiding moon had gone to ground and like the plover
hunting on the shore they relied on movement and sound.

We haggled then as Sargasso seas swam across their irises
and held their stare like the shore guarding the shape it has made,
not giving an inch. They dreamed of eye-bright, speedwell
eye-worth and bluet. We struck the deal,
money like a vision changed hands. They touched the coins
thumbing along the milled edges, weighing them up.

The notes they smoothed out checking the size,
hauling up an image of their worth. Their retinas gave back no shapes
clouded as they were like the surface of water in Autumn.
We checked our purchases held them to our eyes.
looked through the camera's viewfinder, tried the telescope,
were all eyes for the binoculars.

Smoke and Mirrors

The magnifying mirror frames her face
holds tight its reflection, throws it back at her
bright and big. The lens takes her in,
rearranges her face. It is insistent;
a moon drowned in a lake.
It has no point of view, no alchemy except a true
reverse of what it sees. Words fly from her.
The lines on her forehead and at her eyes
are granite. Ogham notched on the sharp edge,
she has become her own memorial stone.

She sees the drowned young girl,
sees that terrible fish swimming towards her.
She steps back past the tideline
her face flips over, a rush of vertigo,
a different point of view flicks into place.
Above the silver arched interior
displaced air is too thin. She has passed
the concave mirror's focal point.
Bell, book and candle cannot hold her.
Suddenly she is Alice, topsy turvy
vanished into a land of smoke and mirrors.

War

The wasps have been murmuring all summer,
now they are garrisoned in the attic
for a last gasp attack. Daily we find bodies
dead or wounded on the bare boards
or stairs. We wear slippers now for fear
of stings. We wonder do they remember
the sun's dazzle as they buzz towards
electric sun lights, then stunned fall back
retreating into oncoming winter.

When we think they have finished their forays
we will climb into the attic, pull our
selves over the ceiling's threshold
into the cold air under the grey slates
and rafters that make up their sky.
We will mop up any stragglers,
seek out the nest, slash and destroy,
head them off from a reconnaissance
this time next year.

The Carrier

I hold my daughter close,
loving the lines of her body.
She carries my fingerprints,
I carry her history.

In the angle of her head,
that I can cup with my two hands,
lies the future.
She will be the death of me.

I carried her below my heart
for nine short months,
she will carry me forever.

I am running along the lines
of her blood. I am tapped
into her bone. I am the echo
in her head.

Matchwood

In the time it takes for the match
to burn to your fingers branding
you for life, tell us your story.

With the smell of sulphur surrounding
you, describe if you can the day
you flew through the air

for a few vital seconds, on roller
skates, having seen the fifties version
of Torvil and Dean and believing

that you too could take flight.
The crash on frozen concrete, when it came,
concentrated your mind and fractured your arm,

cracking with cold. Greenstick, pronounced
the doctor as he festooned it with gauze,
setting it tight in plaster, made us think

of a sapling, the soft wood igniting through
friction involving the air and another hard
surface. Burn, baby burn.

K2 Mountain

i.m. Alison Hargreave mountaineer, died on K2 in 1995.

This summer was so hot
the hills burned.
Mother saw it as a sign,
she said she knew
a cool bright mountain
waiting to be climbed.

Some days she peels the potatoes,
prepares the dinner, tucks us in.
Some days she simply has
to climb a mountain.
When I asked her why,
she said the air down here
is too heavy and the light too dim.

On the mountain the air is thin,
the white snow gleams, she said
she feels nearer heaven.
I have been there too,
she carried me with her
as she clawed up the cliff face.

I heard her heart beat fast,
her breath grow shallow,
I swear I almost saw the light.
But where she carried me
was warm and night dark.
Down here I can only dream
of how the snow gleamed
before it folded her in.

The Terracotta Army

They dug for water and found
the enemy buried there.
In Shaanxi the walls of paper shanties
rustle with stories of evil spirits
sucking water from the arid land.

How light they would have slept,
had they but known that underneath their feet,
his silent comrades stood, eleven columns
facing East. Six thousand men and more

Fashioned from mud, two thousand years
they have stood on feet of clay.

No old men's slippered feet shuffle now
the corridors of Royal Kilmainham,
passing the tag ends of days
recalling former glory in the glow
of well worn brass buttons;
remnants of another army.

I look with eyes unable to perceive
how many ancient worlds had passed
before the army stood large and grey
picked out from shadows on resplendent walls
and footfall deadening carpet.

Quin Shihuang's terracotta army stands
in timeless mockery of the man.

The Cure

As the mist lifts off the fields in the morning,
droplets dry in the air and sparkle
with white water that edges the tide.
As the sea retreats rock pools are exposed,
blue/black clams, tiny orange crabs,
white scalloped shells.
Cup it with your eyes and drink it in.

That last night beside me you cried out
in sleep. 'Bastards. Bastards',
with a venom that belied your daytime face.
Then I saw in your eyes
where too much light has been.
We sit together now, sandpaper people
scratching each other down to bone.

Just before nightfall go down to Spanish Point
and listen, listen to the wash thundering
the rocks. Hear the dark cormorants rustle
among seaweed and hear the long grasses
sigh and settle. Lie and listen until you reach
silence and the demons stop needling
your skin. Don't come in
near the city until you are quiet.

A Body Recovered

As the car wound its way higher up,
off to my left the city sprawled out.
Up here it was mostly bog or bare rock,
along the sides of the narrow road
the sight of singed heather
blended with the brown of the bog.

Occasionally I could see the bent backs
of men footing the turf, leaving it terraced.
Further up the tall television mast
looked like an alien smothered under
low cloud. As I wound round yet another
twist of the road, a strange sight
snagged my eyes. On a thin green
lime road, in full dress stood an undertaker,
his hearse beside him.

His assistant's shouldered the coffin,
whose colour almost blended with the bog.
A knot of policemen stamped their feet
on the ground, the whole scene was surrounded
by tape that waved like bunting in the wind.
I turned the car homewards,
shivering in the fading September heat.
That night as I built the fire up
with brown turf. The flames rose
like a fanfare.

Flying Fish

"A woman needs a man like
a fish needs a bicycle."
                    Irena Dunn

I saw one the other day, tail fins
flashing sunlight off its scales
and you sailing down the street

on your bicycle, peddle pushing
hard. Who ever said a fish can't
fly, has obviously never seen you try.

Swerving off course, your spokes are silver
rods reeling me in, as you dart
by row after row of houses,

the street almost deserted, now floods with
you out of breath and panting, gills working
like bellows. Breathless with love

and desire you swerve to a halt. Stopped,
you are a fish out of water and I,I,I, hooked
goping and gaping, mouth open wide say hello. Hi.

Domestic

My house is full of knives.
Sharp blades wait to ambush me
in drawers. I get sleepy from their cuts.
my onion finger peels back layers,
reveals the blood and guts of me.
Sometimes the trap is on the stairs,
a lost left shoe discarded there
hides like a snare to trip me up.

There's danger in domestic things
such as you would never dream.
Light falling at an awkward angle
can splinter air
like discordant voices.
My head becomes
the tumble dryer's cycle,
round and round it goes.

Weeping Willow

A willow tree hangs like a green tiered wedding cake,
colonised by bindweed its bouquet of white
blooms briefly. Hundreds of Linnets line up
on the electrical cable sensing the message
coming down the line, waiting for the snare of wind
to lift them off as if raising a toast to the sky.
In their search for warmer weather they are rushing
to meet the unknown, like the people
of Cloud-Cuckooland   who tried to capture
the same bird and hold spring forever.

But spring and summer are another continent.
We are heading towards the autumn equinox,
the willow drags its skirts as it leans a little closer
trying to foretell its future. Its confection of bindweed
will blacken and perish going to ground to flourish
in another year. Day and night move to alignment
we sit and watch the lowering sun.
Plants hold their fading flowers, the sweet pea is dying
still staked to cross-threaded bamboo poles.
A late Oriental poppy jettisons it last petal
on the aisle of the herbaceous border
as we prepare to cross the threshold into winter.
Everything is holding its breath.

This is the year of Mars, our rogue warrior brother
closer to us now than he's ever been. Once he was
the harbinger of spring, overtaken now by battle.
Nightly we look to the darkening sky, straining
to catch sight of the red warning,
its twin moons Phobos and Deimos are like bridesmaids
telling of panic and fear. Sometimes we think
we can see its light, or are we misled
like the astronomer Lowell, seeing things
where nothing exists?

Fleeced

The noise of council workmen dragged me
from the computer and left my words flickering
on screen. They had just finished cementing
a patch of pavement and covered it
with a tan-coloured hessian sack to ward off night-frost.
I turned back to the dancing screensaver
rainbows blending their primary colours
while I ransacked my brain for words to fit.

Harsh chattering distracted me, I looked
out my window as the air filled with wings:
a gulp of magpies pulled at the loose weave
of the coarse cloth like veteran gleaners.
The sky was a charm of black and white birds
arriving and departing. Those leaving
carried string streamers in their beaks
– off to festoon their nests.
Within minutes the burlap bag had disappeared,
its only sign a faint crossweave pattern
mixed with crow prints on the drying
concrete. I turned wordlessly back.

from
Dangerous Dresses
(2005)

Landed At Sea

The only thing I can tell you is that
the day we landed on the moon,
It was night here and I was all at sea.
Sailing from Holyhead to Dun Laoire

or was it Dun Laoire to Holyhead
I can't remember which? All I know
is, we spent hours on deck, starboard side
sky gazing as if the speck of moon

had suddenly found its meaning.
We shifted from foot to foot trying to grow
sea legs, keep our balance, ground ourselves,
as the moon in a trick of light
pulled the tide out from under us.

Heart Felt

I saw my heart today, beating, beating
like a bellows, an abattoir river
of blood, thick as a quagmire dredging
through the chambers making room for itself.
The technician captures the clamour on screen,
like an old clavichord player pulling the strings,
she has been to the heart of the matter.
The last time I had a sonograph
there inside me in a small nimbus of light
was a star baby, with ten star fingers.
This time the scan reads more like storm clouds
gathering at the death of day, dark and bloody.

The Arc of a Swing in Autumn

When she is seated
the swing's ropes pull taut
then arc from the ground to the sky,
Chasing the crest of the moon.
Higher and higher she pushes,
branches hold their silence as wind rushes by.
Shadows scatter and are undone.
She goes to ground: displaced air
hauls its light cargo back.

This is her cradle, her sling. Its highs
and lows hold her in a temporary bow
as she spans the distance between grass
and mid-air. She is shattering the light
of the sun, I hold her image framed
I know it is autumn because the leaves are gone.
All I can see is the outline of the tree,
and my mother on the swing
in the time before me.

Stitched

Your scissors flew
ripping all in their path. Inches
and inches of stitches, tied off like butterflies,
the ends going nowhere.

Each one neatly ravelled
as you pulled and sliced at it.
The tapestry pattern that travelled
your leg from ankle to groin

was impressive to my young eye.
The doctor was shocked
as he tried to stop you, but
you were vehement.

They had 'done' your veins,
cut and snipped them
turned them inside out.
A tailor's dummy,

you said you wanted to reclaim
the seams that carry the blood
back to the heart.

The Gates of Horn

(After Sylvia Plath)

I type in Arial to give the words
a breathing space –
open like red tulips
to her hurt lines. Lady Lazarus
in the hospital bed,

doing what she did best, again
and again. Her skin stretched
on a wire frame, O the light,
it was lovely, but it hurt her, the red
was too much.

The tulips almost touched her
with one eye firmly on the sky
looking for the unmiraculous, winged
woman, her stamen rising
to the stings.

Time Traveller

She leans her back into the slats of the chair,
the bars imprisoning her, a pouch holding her in.
The nodes of her backbone strain her skin
and time spools back on a thread.
Her golden head a skull then, bone white,
small enough to fit snug in a hand;
the eye sockets hold the coins
of her green/blue eyes like a purse.

the nub of her heart pulsing like a pinprick,
translucent bud fingers and toes
reaching out past the walls of the womb
grasping her future that has arrived.
She emerged, a human flower,
bright and expected, the kernel of death
sits in under her skin and that skull
will one day be revealed again.

For now she sits with her sea anemone fingers
wrapped around a pencil that she mows
across the white of a page like someone
cutting a lawn in regular sweeps.
She is writing her own story
moving herself into the centre of her life,
not loaned, or copied, or borrowed,
just hers.

Yes, I Can Bake a Cake

("But can she bake a cake?" Asked a newspaper after
Amelia Earhart had flown solo across the Atlantic.)

And sometimes in the aching loneliness
of taut unforgiving sky, she wished she'd stayed
and baked some more. Time bent and blended
into nothing. The engine a soothing sound,
she watched the Vega's instruments and dials
as if their numbered faces would reveal
her soul's dominion. She became a two winged
seraphim flying in heaven's slipstream, that
radar operators logged as angel, mistaking
her for geese blown off course and heading east.

Instead she chose to fly from Harbour Grace
to some unknown place in Ireland.
First landfall after all that blue air and sea,
the pasture beckoned green and grounded.
A few startled cows felt wind rush past
their ears, heard the sound of wings and saw
a red Mayfly go past, touch down. A farmer
stood his ground and greeted her,
said she was in Gallagher's field
and worried would she sour the milk.

Sound Waves

In the drum of my mother's womb
I hear her troubled heartbeat
hammering on an anvil
making it sing.

Bound by the dark,
a spark of sound rings round me
breaking in stars of water.
I hear the insistent beat

of her heart, rhythm of her feet
as she moves, pulling me with her.
Sometimes I hear her sob.
In here I am all ears.

There is no silence,
even when she sleeps her steady rhyme
rises and falls, a metronome
noisy about me.

Child C

I am the child that carries the child,
a Russian doll, a hawthorn hedge.

The flower and the thorn. We are hemmed in
with white flowers. I am a named child

who bloomed early. A May blossom
burgeons inside me.

Above our heads they talk a language;
some mad boolean algebra

in trimesters and letters
that fetter me here.

I was bridging the chasm between
child and woman

when he tore through me, planting
his seed, battering my senses and flesh.

I like a firefly then, burning the bushes
scorching the white blossoms, stripping the bark.

When the bough breaks
we all fall.

Dangerous Dresses

The first time she saw them,
she noted their hair in tight
ringlets for Sunday mass,
saw too the chiffon dresses
whisping in the bitter wind,
white socks and black patent shoes.

Two pretty girls going to mass,
she thought they looked like
dressmakers dummies.
They in turn looked at Raggedy
Ann, eyes locked in mutual contempt

as they assessed her split skirt,
sensible socks and brogues.
Clothes to run and climb in,
clothes to be Annie Oakley in
and they envied her not a bit.

Ann scorned their limb-snaring
tresses and dresses, but lusted
after the patent shoes, not to wear,
but to hoard in crisp tissue
in a box and know they were there.
As for the chiffon, Ann well knew
the dangers in dresses like that.

Yew Trees

This place is mainly peopled with Yew,
their leaves and branches grieve.
Their neat form holds them in place
like the dug grave, only biding its time,
to hold somebody
snug in its tight shoulder.

Salmon on his homeward run
reminds us of bodies gravitating
back into earth. He makes
water ring, his scales speckle
in the light. It was Shrovetide
the traditional marriage day,

Ash Wednesday came and
forty days of fasting followed.
We buried them together,
feet facing the setting sun,
a tide of earth washing over them.
Algal bloom blooms deadly.

Clay shifts and settles, sediment
drops. Our feet crushing the camomile
lawn, its scent released like the show
of white petals of cloudberries.
    "A tisket, a tasket
      a green and yellow basket".

The notes lifting skywards past
the high tide line on the flowered grass,
a tune inherited, a low drone
oscillating between this
and *"Tulips from Amsterdam"*.
Those tunes and your wedding ring,

a golden fish shimmering.
Battered grass and the Yews excessive
green, their shrouded needles piercing us
as we walk past headstones. Marble
and granite studded with lichen,
an occasional wooden cross

nailed at its crosspiece. A name painted,
as if in promise of more permanence.

The Hope Chest

She kept all her treasures in the Hope chest.
The silver tankards from her grandmother,
lace hankies from some cousin or other
and a glass, art nouveau, single rose vase,
delicate lace sewn over many days.
Also starched linen sheets and some cotton
and other pieces almost forgotten.
Everything kept there was the very best.

Over the long years things started to rot.
Grandmother's tankards began to tarnish
with a patina, green like a varnish.
As for the vase, it long ago shattered
the lace it went brown, not that it mattered.
The sheets went limp and fell in on themselves
into her bright future nobody delves,
as for the chest, all but she has forgot.

Tempus Fugit

To where will all this gathered time
bring us, when year after year
a new spring comes followed
by summer and the losses of autumn
and winter cold and hard?
With luck it all goes 'round again.

So can I ask the question yet again?
How else will we gather up our time
some will not make it, and that is hard
our friends get fewer year on year
though some had barely reached autumn.
Some voice called and they followed.

We cry, why do you go, why have you followed
this song you have heard over and over again?
Once summer is done it leads again to autumn
gather your hopes and dreams and keep time
at bay, enter the promise of another year
though sometimes lonely, sometimes hard.

Some went so early they never saw the hard
truth of life that is long, a road followed
through days of fortune, days when the year
could not end soon enough, trials repeated yet again.
Others were wondrous we travelled back in time
to relive a glorious spring, fulfilled by autumn.

Winter clips the heels of mellow autumn
the encroaching cold makes the ground hard
with frost decorating every garden, now is the time
to tend to what has bloomed and followed
from last year and check what will come again
when spring breaks open new ground next year.

Then you welcome gifts you're given every year
our time is marked like the seasons and glories of autumn
remembered in sunny days that come again.
Good friends gathered only in memory is hard
to comprehend. Some day we will have followed
them and another generation will have their time.

Use well your time, as you walk the path your ancestors
    followed
here you are in lush autumn, winter will not be far behind
    and once again
slowing days down will be hard as the flying weeks move
    through the year.

from
Lovely Legs
(2009)

Masks

A man stands in a field wearing a mantle
of bees. He stands very still, the queen
snared in a cage under his chin.
The black/yellow bodies dance
in the sun, they clamour insistently and stay
very close to him. Their intricate patterns
too complex for anyone to follow.

the sun is a monstrance haloing the skies
and fields are still bordered
with hummingbirds' trumpet, spikes
of orange montbretia and healing yarrow.
These are foreign fields, things gone awry.
The sweep and swoop and drone of the bees
tell of the fields and the erratic flowers,
some from as far as Tierra del Fuego.

Midsummer has been and gone;
The man hangs like a golden apple,
as bees tell each other of the scent
of white yarrow; *millefolium* – a thousand
leaves. They map what they see
with diamond eyes, note
just where their queen is, she is the prize
and the man is taking her on the chin.

Elsewhere a woman says she wants
sunflowers on her grave. She loves
their pomp and majesty, wants them
to face her and not the sun,
wants their seeds to fall into the earth,
mingle with her marrow and take root.
The man in the mask of bees moves gingerly,
and with a small shake frees himself and leads
the captive bees back to their frame.

Hooks

Don't look at me with a wide mouth
gaping and full of hooks, fish-like
and carping. Oh I have poems
as yet unsung spun from shifts
in air and the geometry of sky.

Your full mouth may jape and jibe
I am used to you and your capers.
The leap and cavort of your tongue
and your sunken cheeks all strung
with hooks and lines will not reel me in.

I'll set my teeth against the wind
my words will sally out sprang as can be,
your speech is famine talk
don't come at me mealy-mouthed
and grave-talk Irish.

The Docile Girls

Lin-We lives in Zijin Cheng with the other docile girls,
    all young and slender,
with sleek dark hair, they look like Seals when they bathe.
The palace is so large it is a city; the Imperial or Forbidden
    city,
it has many rooms and building and terraces and pavillions.
Lin-We lives in one of the six Eastern palaces.
Except for young Shunzhi our esteemed Emperor no man
    may live here after dark.

In daytime the sun travels from over her building to the
    Western Gate,
past halls paved with golden bricks and on over Golden
    Water river
with its white marble balustrades quarried from Lin-We's
    hometown
of Fang Shan. When the last of the light sinks down
    behind the magnolia trees
all the mandarins and clerks and grooms leave.

At night there are only the docile girls and the eunuchs,
those lost boys, who were docked in the service of the
    Divine Emperor.
Lin-We thought her lot was better, there were so many
    other girls here
that the young Emperor had only visited her twice.
On those nights the other docile girls prattled excitedly
as they brushed her hair and freshened her breath and
    teeth with bark,
they lay her on a bed perfumed with rose petals.
The scent was so strong she fell into a torpor.

The Emperor stroked her face and thighs and praised her,
he called her his Lotus Blossom. All the girls knew that flower
and how it only bloomed its waxy, luminous flower for
    one short day.

When Emperor Shunzhi left her bed the palace sent her
        mother golden coins
with his face stamped on them as Lin-We had felt his
        weight imprinted on her and felt
again his manhood enter her. She thought about how at night
there is only one penis in the whole palace.

She daydreamed about how someday she would like to
        walk along
the Imperial Way, but knew no woman may do so except
        an Empress
on her wedding day and even then she must watch her
        steps very carefully.

Prevailing Winds

We listen closely to the radio now
for ways of foretelling the weather,
we watch for the hunkering down of cows.

The man who came about the boiler
said the prevailing wind is south westerly.
He seemed to know which way it blows.

It comes snorting and howling
like a stamping beast across the flat
of the bog scattering everything,

even our thoughts before it.
Wind lifts the earth from the lazy beds,
some days it carries the smell of the sea.

Yesterday I found a tiny shell nestled
amongst the gravel, I read the signs
and know how far it travelled.

I could tell what was coming by the way
swallows are tossed to the lee of the house.
The wind unravels words, our tongues are locked.

Our main concern used to be traffic news;
which junction and where was blocked
by the volume of cars?

Here everything is tied down
even on clear days we scan the skies
the seigh mentality — our little civil wars.

Uncharted Lanes

We could travel all the redbrick lanes
behind houses in roads with names like;
Palmerston, Windsor or Ormond
they had no ordinance, did not appear on maps
or not the ones we were using, we could spy into the backs
of houses that from the front gave nothing away.
Here were old shed doors painted cherry red or apple green
or galvanised steel garage doors that went 'up and over'.
From where we walked we could see into scullery windows
and gardens that grew apple trees, or bushes of gooseberries
or trees with swings hung from them.
Some garden's sported a snagged tennis net.

Sometimes we'd see a pond overgrown with mossy
stones half submerged and we could spy
into a garden shed, its cobwebbed junk taking
on a significance not found in our own sheds.
That cardboard box with faded writing
must contain something more precious than old/
new kitchen tiles that were surplus to requirements.
We liked the uncharted lanes and byways, only children
and dogs in a hurry used them. Once a terrible man,
dressed in a Greatcoat and wheeling a bicycle came along,
he had one hand on the saddle and the other tugged
at his swollen member. This made us remember
to hurry home for tea. We never spoke about it later
and never told our mothers, we would not have had the words.

Shaping Water

Water's translucent
silkiness shapes itself
around the stone
droplets form as
the woman washes
at the basin cupping
her hands in water
that slides over her
and ripples on the orbs
of her breasts
cascades onto the round
of her stomach
flows in the v
between her lovely legs
pools in her toes
sun slants through
the glass gilding her
in splashes of light
she is a body of clear water.

Vitreous China

I locked my young self in the bathroom
forgot the lock was rusty and when the snip went
over, that was that, it could not be pulled back.
No-one had missed me, so I rummaged
in the cabinet and found what I was after,
my father's razor. Too small to reach
the mirror, I copied him by touch,
drawing the blade backwards and forwards
across my face, tapping the lethal steel
on the side of the basin that I always
thought said Virtuous China, and made
it sing like I had seen him do.
Then a strong stinging sensation
on my skin, it hurt and I wailed.
Mother came running and tried to get in,
but the door held. Eventually
father shouldered it, the lock gave
and they came crashing through.
I can still hear her roar as she saw
my face crisscrossed and dripping
with blood. Only then did I remember
that girls don't shave.

Fighting Talk

The bright lie togs itself out
in the yellow racemes of laburnum –
a lemon surprise to trap birds and flies,
it spreads its poison gift wrapped.

Truth is a labyrinth, obscured
like the alburnum that lies between
the sapwood and the heartwood
we sense it just below the surface.
The hard outer bark, a polished lustre,
something lacquered over.

When we strip it down;
flense it with our vowels
and diphthongs,
flay it with words
and recite it,
write it endlessly out,
gloss it,
parse it,
in the worm of our tongues
it still spells out war.

Before

This is a girl of seventeen, a side view,
seated on a swing
hung from a chestnut tree
her dress hitched by the wind

This is a picture of my mother
before I was her daughter
before her father disowned her
before she married my father
before she had six children

This was all before the swinging sixties
that could not free her
before the doctors
before the hospital stays grew longer
and longer,

before they fed the electricity
into her poor head that failed to help her
before the priest offered prayer as a cure
before the shock of her own mother's death
hit home

This is my mother before I saw her
dead in the bed, her cold hands
clutching at air,
before life swung full circle
and could no longer hold her

This is her on that green day
skirt askew, hair streaming out,
holding the ropes of the swing taut
rushing to meet her future
arcing in the air before her.

Scandinavian Dream

The dead visit me in dreams
as I lapse between consciousness
and sleep, in that hazy ante-room
where dreams are hung waiting
to be tried on.

Lately my father has come to me,
alive and well it seems after all.
He now lives near some Scandinavian
forest, in a bright log cabin. I see bark
peel from the burnished wood
and trees in the middle distance,
a small clearing like a yard
outside the door with honeysuckle
growing under the eaves.
I could describe this place
enough to go there if need.

The air here is light and suffused
with motes that could be fireflies
waiting for the dark to illuminate them.
My father does not speak to me,
though he is sentient I know,
nor seems to notice I am here.
He looks my way but his gaze goes
right through me. He rests
on an upholstered chair,
with orange birds of paradise
embroidered on the upright,
this intricate pattern looks out of place here
where everything is pared down and
uncomplicated. Even if he no longer
knows me, I am glad I have seen him,
and that he is content, death suits him in some way.

At daybreak my husband gently touches me
I leave the woods and wake to the summer
cotton counterpane on our bed,
the radio murmuring some unwelcome news.
I fix my sleep filled gaze on a trapped butterfly
tapping its morse unanswered on the window pane.

Cardioversion

'Cardioversion is a medical term for trying to correct the heart's
rhythm with the use of electric shocks.

(For Dr. Peter Quigley)

Sunk in Faraday's Dark Space I try to float
upwards, struggle through layers of ether drift
to blazing light. The air zings with shock,
I am charged, jolted, I have mislaid my beat, its loss
has grounded me, a wild horse, I buck and snort,
leaping as they apply the branding iron that sears
my skin with an unexpected rhythm. They count
the volts, they scorch me and try again with pads
that arc blue electricity from front to back
as it travels the long way through my heart
it stops   and   starts
whipping up a corona of light an aurora borealis
that does not augur well. A runaway horse
I bolt, kick the traces and take flight,
                    I cannot
                        get in synch.

Back in the ward the Doctor appears like Elector
arcs of light beam out from behind his head.
I shy away. The Doctor he says, that between
the two sharp angles of each shoulder blade
is a perfect half circle, a horseshoe shape
of raised red skin. Now as it heals
it itches in a place
                    I cannot reach.

The Stolen Sheela-Ná-Gig of Aghagower Speaks

Set high above the doorway, under the flying buttress
pockmarked now with age and lately turned to stone,
I sat. Know me I whisper, I am woman, I am crone
With my etched lashless eyes, hairless head,
grinning mouth and triangular nose how could I tempt
    anyone?
The wind and rain are always at me, lashing me,
leaving me lonely. Someone saw me and desired me,
swayed by my crude posturing, my endless fertility.
When I open my thighs the world flows in
and the world flows out. I have spent all my life
so far exposed above Aghagower perched in place
knowing the world through the spread of my lips.
In the unconditional dark someone dethroned me,
un-croned me, made me young and beautiful again.
I shrieked leave me be, I am happy.

from
Merman
(2012)

Left Over Christmas Trees

Paper never refuses ink,
no matter how hard the words
it just absorbs. In the same way
the eye never refuses the blue
of sky, the fish water, the bird
never spurns air.

In the wind eucalyptus leaves
show their silver undersides,
you can predict rainbow weather
by the way light flattens itself
and turns chrome, or like
metal filings and lake-water it looks
dense and eloquent as mercury.

Against the bow of colours
birds are tossed about and luff off
into a wreath of gathering darkness.
Passing a forest in January
left over Christmas trees
stand rootless, bound tight
in shrouds of white netting,
swaddled in failing light
they look sinister, grey people emerging,
the sequence of time slipping.
I drove on – my wheels welcoming
the tarmac and the journey home.

Fragments

(A whirring of wings down the sky)

We will start with Sappho:
Love shook my heart
like the wind on the mountain
troubling the oak trees.

My oak tree is troubled, my husband
out gallivanting on the ride-on-mower
broke three years of green growth,
a clean snap, the sap stopped rising.
I tend its wound, retie the black halter.

There is an venerable oak on Elba,
or Isola de Elba as Napoleon knew it
when he sought shade from the boiling
sun under its nurturing arms.
When sailing the Tyrrhenian sea
having lately left the coast of Amalfi
I thought I spied its uppermost branches.

Be just, my lovely swain, and do not take
Freedoms you'll not to me allow, said Aphra Bhenn,
not playing any games, agent 160
as she was also named. She revealed
the DeWitts' plan to burn wooden ships
docked in the Thames.

This was transmigration indeed, never
mind the souls who sail the seven seas.
In a mangrove swamp of eerie trees,
roots exposed and everywhere grey mud
oozed and the world decomposed while we watched
our step on slippery boards.

In another light Aurora Borealis flashed
its pea green glow about the sky. Adam and
Eve stand in a hum of desire under an oak tree
whispering about how it was all going to be DNA
from that day forth.

my mother never had a television, fridge, or phone,
didn't ever dream of mobiles, computers,
iPods. Now our houses are full of bytes and modems,
at night the LED lights glow. When anything breaks
it is replaced, we go shopping,

to sail on silver moving stairs that buckle and repeat
up to the novel and new. In a Chinese whisper of need
we view motionless mannequins whose mouths
are stopped in a wordless O, then push through
other shoppers like swimmers in a crowded pool,
afraid we are on collision course and that we
might glance the arm or leg of a fellow swimmer.

Inside the dream the glittering coffee machines
are lined up like the Red Army advancing.
While we finger Venetian crystal,
the espressos hiss alarm and steam
as if the trembling glass held hemlock
and not just air, albeit expensive air;
we look blank as mannequins.
Again I think of my mother and the enduring oak
of my family tree, how quickly we leave all but our DNA.

Out again into the market place and busy streets,
at the end of Henry Street stands the Spire;
our soaring homage to the god of commerce and of sky;
its pinnacle thin as the wood of the spindle tree.
Outlined against bright sky, a giant steel needle
daily stitches the heavens and this earth together.
Tomorrow is the first day of Lent,
who will be first to renounce the virtual chorus
and silence the tweets and calls,
lose the constant contact we have through the waves
and like the swimmers or indeed Adam and Eve
reject the void and brush against the flesh
of one another?

Tell me what now, above all,
your frantic heart desires.

Whatever the Weather

The day after the storm we noticed water
reaching right up to the flood
mark. With the receding morning tide
it had drawn back the line against
bladderwrack thrown up by stormy weather;
weed and debris on the beach sparkled in light.

When morning filled the room with light
we woke from dreams of water
tuned in the radio to hear the weather.
An announcer talked about the flood
while we entangled our sleepy limbs against
the bed end, holding back the tide.

We are late. A quick tumble will have to tide
us over; you rain kisses light
on me and hold me close against
your chest. Outside the sea is at low-water
hundreds of hungry gulls flood
the sand, for the booty of stormy weather.

Marriages made on earth have to weather
the daily flotsam of a running tide,
sometimes old arguments threaten to flood
back and we try to keep conversations light.
Currents of riptides do not hold water
when we have things to kick against.

Put in this backdrop, landscape against
the joys and trials of marriage can be heavy weather.
Years can pass like so much water
flowing under a bridge; small comforts tide
us over. Passion ebbs but light
can be brought to bear when memories flood.

Outside remains of yesterday's flood
throw rainy squalls hard against
the window, sometimes obscuring light.
It is like marriage, this constantly changing weather.
Our children are almost grown, then a turning tide
will favour us to float our boat in calmer water.

Now let our lives flood with undiminished light
and do not worry whether or not, we row against
the tide, we are happy to have dipped our toes in the water.

Merman

I had been working in the fish farm for weeks,
that one near the river outlet and the sea.
I didn't like the work we were constantly
wet, dirty, didn't like the men there either.
They were insolent, often dropped small fry
and crushed them underfoot. One in particular
Glaucus, tall, muscular cast his sea-green eyes over me,
tried to lure me as I tipped phosphorus feed
into the holding pens that smoked and stank
and made mist veils I tried to hide within.

One day he walked towards the tanks
waders held in his large hands, he was chewing
on a herb he said was magical, always urging
me to eat it. I would not bite. Anyway whatever way
it was, he leaned to pull the waders on, both legs
got caught in one boot and over he flipped.
I cast around for help, no-one was there. I went back.
He was emerging from amongst the shoals
of salmon, clinging to his single wader
up to his waist were the glittering scales of smolts.

He rose shaking, coloured sequins waterfalling
as he tried to right himself and beckoned me for help.
I took the bait and when I caught him,
we stumbled, he landed me and pinned me down,
I looked, held his eyes, it was early the rising sun
was flooding them with hooks of golden light. I said No.
He parted my thighs and when it was over,
untangled his legs, shook the silver armour
from himself, his eyes had lost their lustre.

I left distraught and walked all day stumbling
over ditches and hillocks, stopped now and then
to eat, following the river to its source.
At so many hundred feet I rested where the stream
welled from the earth, cooled my toes, kicked gravel

into little pools and felt the flow snagging
in the waters of my womb. I cried and screamed
and shook my fists at the sky, knew then this birthing
pool was to be my fate, tried to obliterate
his sea-green eyes, his face, his terrible merman tail.

Decorating

A ladder's silver legs ascending
and descending, me straddling
the summit. Specks of paint flake our eyes
as together we go at stripping the walls
slicking a sweat which reminds me
of the old delight that springs back
and glosses into life. Brushes
converging in an urgency
of now perform a choreographed
dance,   slow,   slow,

quick, quick,
                    slow
pulsing light across the waiting walls.
Air thrums taut as a newly skinned drum;
dusty scraps of waxy moths beat time
on the double glazing clouding it—
a small weather front patterning
the window glass. Your hands brushing
my skin colouring it in dappled light,
Water Lilly White flaring
like the Aluminium ladder rungs; paints spilt
and left pooling on the floor.

Skinny Dipping

I'm Irish, we keep our clothes on
most of the time. We perform
contorted dances on beaches in Cork,
or Donegal; undressing under
not-yet-wet-towels. Worried that any gap
might expose us, lay some body-part bare.
It was the Immaculate Conception that did it,
if Mary could conceive a child without
removing her knickers, then by God
the rest of us could undress and swim
without baring our buttocks.
We swam serene in freezing seas,
goose bumps freckling our pale skin.
We lay togged out on wet sand desperate
for the weak sun to dry us, before performing
the contorted dance in reverse. Now as I
remove my clothes, peel them off
layer by layer down to the bare,
a brief moment of unease before the release
of water baptising skin. With a quiet 'Jesus, Mary',
I dive in.

My Mother Ate Electricity

Sometimes, on stormy nights, I think of you
how death persuaded you in increments
and not as a bolt out of the blue.
Your mind a landscape blazing with bushfires
until they nailed you in place, fed volts
into your brain and bound it up in haywire.
Said they cleared the mists, didn't tell
of the smoke shrouding your eyes.

Opiates lay like wafers on your tongue,
all the black hate gone, as were the songs
and memories; babies caged in cots
waited for your care, our endless cries
seared your brain until the doctor applied
the shocks again and again, whitened your bones
and cauterised the sound. The babies called
as if from an oubliette and you left
eating handfuls of forgetting.

The Backward Step

We need to wind things back,
put time in reverse, loop the ravelled
ribbon, fill the spool with thread again.
We need to empty out your grave,
backfill the hole that gaped,
spit out the Obol and let the wind restring
your voice with new, clear breath.
I will leave the blizzard of your still body
coffined on the table in the living room,
undo the shroud pins and remove
the brown Franciscan robe.
Who's idea was that anyway?

Let us start that day over.
No fight from me this time when you drive
up on your motor scooter, your short hair
helmeted around you to where I wait;
a bad tempered teenager at a bus stop.
I will draw my unicorn horn back in,
turn my cheek the other way
and receive your healing kiss. We will sit
in the June sun together in our summer frocks
and restring the beads of all the lives
that warped to accommodate your loss.
You will live to a fine old age,
and I, your daughter, will in turn mother you.

Hatching The Vision

On the embossed wallpaper
in my daughter's room
pages torn from a school atlas
are pinned to the furred design.
Arrows curve across countries and seas,
a life lived forward. A frieze
of laurel leaves decorate the borders,
she is trying to gain some traction
on the wide world, find her footing.
No atlas moth can eat holes in her,
no moss will gather, she is on the move,
a stone rolling. Her cocoon walls
are expanding, next the roof might take off
and sail to far-flung places.

The looped lines cleave the atlas
like swallows slicing evening air;
or a sword loose from its scabbard
carving the world into manageable pieces
out beyond its frame of shining leaves
and stitching them into the wide clear blue.
With wind in her pockets the trajectory
of those pointing arrows are aiming
at a future for now just visualised.
They say clearly as any cartography:
I'm outta here.

Hinamatsuri

Nusha, our daughter loves the ceremony of the dolls,
the prince and princess seated in tiered splendour,
the loving couple at the apex, lolling like melons
with their robes puffed out around them,
painted faces almost smiling, lacquered lips red as cinnabar,
their night-dark hair is real and shines as if lit by stars.
Nusha brushes her hair until it glows, taps her wooden *getas*,
wriggles her toes. This is her day for praise and future-wish
our job is to guide her, watch her grow and push
her off into the river of life, like the dolls of long ago.
Ever year we stow them away, no longer made of straw,
but something more substantial, something lasting.

The next row seats five musicians, garb not as sumptuous,
as royalty, but gorgeous nonetheless, each one holds
an instrument that Nusha says she can hear, hear the strings,
hear them sing. Our ears are too old for such sounds;
we listen as leaves rustle in trees, and a tumult of traffic goes by.
The last step holds the helpers, clothes more like our own *Yukatas*;
plain, servicable. They proffer the food, mochi sweets, peach
blossoms, brushes for the royal couple's hair, oils and unguents.
Nusha holds a western doll, tall with golden hair, slim waist,
generous chest, she says I need to grow up soon, it's urgent.

Blue Bobbin

Its dull case an ornament
in the corner, its use almost
forgotten. someone has taken
the table of the Singer Sewing
machine, once everyone had one.
If you lifted it out you could turn
the handle instead of footing
the treadle. Gone, along
with the table is the drawer
that held bobbins, my delight,
as a child sifting the
spools of rainbow thread.

When my mother sewed
she favoured the blue bobbin.
All our curtains, whatever the colour,
were backed with blue stitches.
I helped her thread the needle
through a maze of eyes and hooks
down to where the thread vanished
into a small silver box.
Like a magician pulling an endless
stream of hankies from his sleeve;
it conjured another thread
and together, they and we,
formed the stitch.

At night when mother was busy
I used to slide the lid on the silver
chamber to see if I could figure out its trick.
I only saw the small half-moon lever
moving back and over
and like a hidden slice of sky,
the edge of a blue bobbin peeping out.

The Mirror Demons

(from a poem by Adrienne Rich)

She watched herself
  noticed her reflection
    kept subtly changing.

Nothing sudden
  just an imperceptible
    drawing down

Of the lids of her eyes,
  the flesh of her lips.
    Sometimes, caught unaware

She wondered who
  that woman was,
    that woman

with no lover at her
  shoulder, jeered
    by the mirror demons.

ii

My daughter and her mirror
  court each other daily
    mirrors love to flirt with youth,

it nibbles away at her
  feeds from her day by day
    and unnoticed takes more and more away.

She dances before it oblivious
  twisting and turning in its flattering light,
    it only reflects truth, at heart

it is pitiless and impervious
   to the grandeur of her self regard
      its tawdry tinsel light merely observes.

The mirror tells us how we see ourselves
   I want to warn my lovely daughter
      tell her of its jealousy and how it thieves.

iii

Once I bathed in the quicksilver lake
   brushed out my yellow hair
      saw my reflection first thing

every morning, last thing at night.
   Now its searing vision threatens
      to undo me. Now I dread

Its lustre and stand unmasked
   before its crackled glaze.
      My image is brought sharply

into focus, I cringe from its unforgiving
   gaze, seeing only fragments,
      a mosaic of unremembered years,

I drown in its burnished sheen.
   Lift me like the blue/green iridescence
      in the speculum of a bird's wing.

iv

They need to look again
   these people who reflect in me
      blocking my ceiling sky.

All I do is take in the light
   that hits me and bounce it back.
      Like most, I have my demons,

but they are mine and I deal with them.
　　Other than an occasional silver sigh
　　　　I play dumb, like a good host

I try to be discreet, what am I supposed
　　to do? I am mercurial surely they can
　　　　appreciate I have my own truths to tell,

don't ask I say if you can't take it. I only repeat
　　what I see, neither more nor less.
　　　　There is nothing in this for me.

Watching for the Comet

"...for the path of comets is the path of poets:
they burn without warning..."
                                        Marina Tsvetaeva

Towards the west a small celestial trail
spirals the sky and nets me, Jubilant
stars in its wake so pinprick bright
I could trace them with my fingertips,

Their old, cold light clusters like a chorus
chanting for the dead, all my kith and kin,
known and unknown tailing their light for me
to read in the night sky.

My head heavy like a newborn as I
stargaze. I see venus, earth's sister
and I see the lemon moon's
pale slice. Then I feel earth's grip

slip from me, I am unhitched, no longer bound,
I lose my bearing in a sea of fiery stars.
Floating in the firmament I have become
an adumbrated body of falling light.

New Poems

(2013–2016)

Memory Wintering

(for Sheila)

Light contracts
in shorten-
ing days,
a blue moon is rising and you are tearing up
                                        inside.
Roiling in your mind all the poems, made and un-
                                        made
like a strewn bed, sheets rumpled, rancid from too much love.

      The winnowing of memories that flood the brain,
make of you a time traveller, an argonaut
    traveling back through steep
                            steps
                                    of air
      to Sandymount and the   drift of sea,
your father taking you to the opera.
All your siblings set sail for Canada.

      Solid earth gone from under-
                            foot
this is not that country
it is all sea and sky from now on.
Your windows over-
      look St. Stephen's Green,
        two storeys up your eye-line is level
  with ruined light pooling in the tops of trees
      whose leaves by burning leaf
                            drop

   unfastened from their branches

inaudible to our ears as the cry of the soprano pipistrelle
(maybe in this Chora or space you can hear their cacophony),
as whorls of words unspool and the blade of new moon

is clasped in the cradle of the old.

This November two moons are rising
                    like sunstruck sirens causing tumult and
        turbulence
                    and high above cumulus clouds

        e x p a n d i n g,

                    their puffed up fluid whiteness climbing
                                        the sky
and every night without exception
indifferent stars are pulsing everywhere.

Senior Science

The bird skeleton in formaldehyde
drew me in, tiny bones yellowing,
egg-shaped head bald and featherless,
flightless wings permanently tucked up,
and the blue upright flame of the Bunsen burner
a votive candle for the godless,
offering its heat in the service
and sacrifice of science.

Junior, I joined the seniors, slipped
into the back of the busy class,
the teacher never noticed me.
This was way more interesting
than parsing a dead language
or conjugating a French verb. This class
had its complex codes and siftings
and its own dead to parse and puzzle.

Pipettes and Petri dishes, de-
composition and decay.
We worked to solve the riddle
of prolific frogs, Uncurled their slimy legs
and pinned them Christ-like
to a table, pale abdomen exposed.
We stripped the minute broken body
and dissolved its gilding of waxy flesh.

The class found and made solutions,
in Pyrex glass flasks and fretted ugly dogfish,
miniature sharks who laid their eggs in devils' purses.
We were almost alchemists casting golden pennies.
See the wealth of vertebrae, femur,
the phalangeal formula 2-3-3-3-3 of fingers and toes.
We drained lab rats' blood to reach their cherry hearts.
Dealing death was easy then in Senior Science class.

The Troubled Sky

Through a haloed lozenge of window,
we view the Appalachian mountains far below
a rocky range of valleys and troughs
settled with snow reflect Daliesque
clouds pocking the sky.

Inside we are cocooned in pools of light,
our own air blower creating an illusion
of interior weather. Unconcerned
with the Codex on the flight of Birds
we are as children wondering

when the coifed and suited hostess will feed
and water us; when will the disembodied voice
grant us permission to unbuckle seat-belts
and take to the aisle for the short walk
to the cramped stall, there is nowhere else to go.

We left our usual worries thousands of feet down
on the ground, as if stepping out of our skin
or pull of gravity. Large shadows on the wing-tip
retracting and lengthening with every bank and dip
fly us into sunset's crimson arms.

Here we have shifts of time, Tyche, goddess
of chance visits our troubled sleep.
Certainties are upended, we cannot depend
on sunrise in the east, birds flying south
in winter, the fixed north star, prayer even.

Snow in May

Ashy snow falls steadily in dove grey flurries
air folds and collapses like a concertina.
This September, the day is warm,
no sign of cold or snow just the usual
flow of traffic downtown in any city,
horns honk, bells ring, sirens alarm.
And I can remember snow in May.

Grey ash falls in the tortuous air.
the sun is shrouded, in Lower Manhattan
blanketing snow obliterates shapes,
outlines become signs we cannot read.
The sky is thick autumn air laden
with flocks of midges, and the scent of something
spoiling in an orchard, boughs of trees
weighted down with swollen fruit.
And I can remember snow in May.

Later we will stand forehead and hands
against the glass sarcophagus, while
traffic goes howling down the streets,
we see the abyss, the rent in the earth
down to bare bedrock.

In the iron light our minds fill the gap,
the absent towers are made whole again,
windows glint in sunlight, or grey with winter rain
or how we now remember them
as we saw them again,
                                and again.
Grainy on the television screen,

```
ha              ha
If              If
fal             stand
ling,           ing
```

contorted – choking smoke billows into the darkening sky
and we see wave after wave of paper flakes,
fragments that fall like ballast, leap like grief,
each one unique, and I can remember snow...

Schrödinger's Cat-Entanglement

It is very dark in here
and even though people think
I can see in the dark, it's not true
there has to be some thin scrim of light for me.
I only accepted being put in this box
for a morsel of fish.
Like a fool I purred my pleasure
and let him pet me in,
him muttering about energy level of atoms
and wave like properties of particles.
I prefer it when he studies his books
and tinkers with his glass tubes and trays,
leaves me sleeping undisturbed under his desk.
The only sound in this total darkness is Schubert,
he always plays Schubert; *Death and the Maiden*
the strings plucked just like a death knell.
After a bit in this pitch black he lifts the lid. *Voila.*
Like he had performed some magician's
clever trick. The others applaud
when I, not knowing if I were dead or alive,
leapt out, three down, six to go,
I'll not be fooled so easily again.

Back to Basics

On the radio today played a voice I knew,
last heard it was urging me to work harder.
Deep tones that hushed me though
that long ago troubled night, now spread
about my bedroom where just dressed
I check my wardrobe for stashed
Christmas presents.
Check the Santa stocking
with my now-grown daughter's name.
While our male midwife's soothing voice
seems to urge us on again, to heal the rifts
between teenage daughters and mothers
and bring us back to basics,
to that shimmering May night where I hear
again his insistent voice.
Push now, push on past the pain.

Letter To My Darling Daughter

I remember one of our earliest partings,
first day in creche, you were so little
that the minder kept you on her knee.
Then starting school; I have a photo –
you in the yard, a blue pinafore
navy mary-janes on your feet, A rucksack
on your narrow back.

You never looked around as I left,
it was hard not to turn and snatch you away.
Now here we are again, performing
the goodbye ritual we have been perfecting.
You stand with bags hefted across your shoulders,
This time boarding school.
No more running to meet me at the bell,
no breathless rush of ...*and teacher said*...

Now we are both older and when I arrive
to collect you, you shout hurried goodbyes
to girls you live with every day,
while my time with you is meted out,
I cannot complain, it was I who started this,
this sending you away.

Rebel, Rebel

Someone mentioned she has a tattoo,
I think of her soft midriff
the small indent, our life-link at birth.
Perhaps the blank vellum of her back,
where skin is a taut drum stretched
over nubs of budding shoulder blades
wings waiting to grow and fly.
A picture or script? I hope it is script,
written in copperplate for her, for all of us.
My father brought home lead type-slugs
small columns with letters topping them.
They fascinated us as children, we inked them up
and stamped them on everything. Our home
became a place of random letters.
In the turn of my daughter's slender wrist I see it,
the title of a Bowie song from the seventies.
I picture the tattooist with his steel needle
furrowing the blue veins tracking the thin skin
as he ploughs and plants his blue/black
indelible ink careful not to dig too deep,
cause a bleed, *It hurts* she says.

The Jay's Egg

Nestled thick in pine needles and yellowing leaves
on the forest floor, a speckled egg, flawless
as the day it was laid. Melon shaped,
its bluish green shell once held the promise
of translucent feathering bones.
Biding its time, heat slowly seeps from it
as water seeps unbidden into bog holes.

Tips of light decant through walls of tall pine,
and blue of Douglas fir with cones dangling
as votive offerings, sky is a domed roof.
The rust deep of trees is swallowing light,
like a man sucking an egg, yoke and glair
out through a minute hole he has made
leaving the egg to fool the bird that laid it.

But not this egg, this tiny tragedy, wind rocked,
it must have fallen from a height;
though still looking unscathed,
cradled as it was by soft green needle tips.
The heart of this wood seems quiet, serene even,
but is alert, almost ticking. This is a self-contained world,
the world outside riven and volatile,

wind sluices through branches thick with shadows
like water purling over stones, shaping them.
The sun-blocked leafless lower limbs
are skeletal, stripped ribs hanging
from the spine trunks of the trees.
In the loosening tangle of night
the muffled blood bark of fox startles us

the owl's flare of feathers and grapnel claws
appal. Tonight and every night,
death's fine dust is everywhere.
Busy spiders are spinning their way around
this forest, while a blur of squirrels is hell bent

among the branches, pine martens snuffling
the undergrowth and the scrabbling of mice are constant.

This slowly calcifying Jay's egg lies
like an unopened freckled geode,
bedded in the sweet scent of pine
and stink of rotting leaves.
Ordinary on the outside
yet hidden within,
is a hardening heart.

Transit

Somewhere along the line on the chunnel train
from Paris to London the windows turn mirror,
a sign that we have entered the tunnel.
We lean into vaulted walls as we stream by
unaware of weather, day or night, anything really,
except this silver lit tube
barrelling us across unseen borders.

I saw pictures of the huge machine boring its way,
with no room for error through the fragile
chalk and clay of Kent and under the seabed.
Another of men either side of the brink
shaking hands after drilling through the thin membrane
to one-another, in underwater détente.

Best not to think of the thousands of tons
of surging seawater bearing down on us,
in this black hole where no stars shine
and pulsars are light years away.
We ache with the weight of remembered water
and navigate on pre-ordained lines
as the silver thread we travel in unspools
always on the straight and narrow.
Better to sip coffee and watch our endlessly
reflected faces recede in nautical miles of mirror.

Imagine instead gills pulsing through our dimpled skin
as if breathing in the waters of the womb.
We are as migrating fish seeking home to the tune
of the catechism of announcements coming and going
in the digitised voice, fizzing with static
that could be Hal's electronic sister
both anchoring and urging us on our Odyssey
while cautioning. Mind The Gap.

Bushfire – New South Wales

In this heat humans and animals die.
At over forty degrees come the bushfires,
fire sears in leaps and bounds the grassy tussocks
between the blackened mop-top trees.
flying foxes swaddled inside their coat of leather wings, swelter,
baby marsupials boil in their mother's pockets.
Once slithering snakes now writhing hot rods on charred earth,
crickets and grasshoppers pulse and fizz, green popcorn in this burn.

The barometer's thin spine of silver surges up the glass
and the slim line of mercury almost spills out.
Orange and lemon trees fanned by a flaming breeze
have their fruits boiled to a tattered mush of clotted jam,
slip-sliming the ground and ambering insects and flies
that try to outrun or outfly, on singed gauzy wings,
this cremation, ruinous in its reach. Golden wattle's whistle
rises to a screech as flocks of parrots drop,
pea-green tragedies back to cauterised earth.

and the stink of ghost gum eucalyptus, its resin
a crackling river fills our guts, while the drone
of giant aluminium bucket planes weighed down
with precious water to douse the conflagration
drenches the blackened sky. The lost horizon
curls and flares somewhere out of sight. We dream
of river mud, lake water, blue dots of pools in yards,
of rain tattooing our stretched skin as Lazarus-like we dread
the stone stare and mocking of tomorrow's rising sun.

The Stubble Field

A tawny fox stands exposed
in the same stubble field
that last year I walked through
as ears of wheat waved and lifted
waist-high about me. Leaving me
stranded half-woman, half swaying
wheat. He trots alert in the reaped
field that stretches hugely away,
sunlight sets the rough tufted stalks
a-sparkle, he turns flailing
at an imaginary crossroad
as if the shorn wheat still billowed
around him. He pauses, sniffs the air
adjusting to the slow accumulation of loss.

We gun the car down the empty early morning
road, tarmac not yet warmed up.
The fox with nowhere to hide shelters
in studied indifference, betrayed by the rise
of fur bristling at his neck. And I recall
pushing through the fluid wheat, ripping
sticky cobwebs from my bare knees,
unable to see my feet in the dense growth:
yet sensing something, some unease
lifting my hair at the nape. We speed by,
leaving the limitations and losses
of the landscape in the mirror
as the fox zig zags across the stippled
field and we all high tail it out of there.

Breaking The Rainbow

The small flare of the firefly dancing and weaving
and you walking those shiny linoleum corridors.
Rags of hands twisting together, your throat raw
from the purple and pink, the yellow and blue tablets
that the white coated doctors carefully measure out.
Father reassuring with a lie that you would be home soon.
The chemical smell of you, that later would
smell like the lab at school when we fooled
around with compounds and flicked our fingers
in and out of the blue flame of the Bursen Burner
to feel the heat, feel how it might have felt
when they anointed and annealed you.
Weeks or months later the tin men send you home
to mother us, quiet and meek with only a haze of stars
in your grey eyes and the slight shake
of your hands giving it away. Charged you tried
and tried to earth yourself and play Good Wife,
Good Mother and failing on all fronts you collected
the rainbow of tablets from their bottles and jars
and like Antigone choose your own moment.

Moonstruck Generation

(i.m. Neil Armstrong 2012)

Born after the unhinging of war and
before the Cuban Missile crisis,
those weeks when we counted not in days and hours,
but minutes and brushed so close to disaster.
Ever after we looked to the sky at night,
for the face of the yellow moon
watching over us, like a hovering
older sister, paler than day's bright sun.

The dark sky pinpricked with starlight
drew us to it, we knew little of computers;
but knew our silvery steadfast moon,
her coming and going, the way she rode
the sky from dusk to dawn from crest
to horizon, how sometimes in early morning
both planets could be seen at once.
We were going there.

Excitement orbited the days and hours to countdown,
all watched agog the precise preparations,
saw that amazing spaceship and felt we knew
the earthlings who flew it. They blasted off,
exited earth's atmosphere, left us bereft for days
with craned necks we tracked their progress
let loose from our world they bivouacked
on the Sea of Tranquility.

Grounded, children flew cereal box cutouts,
practised hopping as if released from gravity
though staying always on the frequency of home.
In that eight day week we could have sworn
Apollo 11 appeared like a clear vision
coursing steadily for its feisty prize,
but logged only a tumult of stars.
Collectively we released our breath
when they splashed back from the blue
into the Pacific and appeared to walk on water.

Out Of His Element

If he could fly he would go now
to his spawning pool, instead he
lies drowning in air,
his glistering
iridescent scales dulling down.
His eyes grow cold and flat
clouding over, the leap and struggle
ended. One leap too far and he landed
on earth stranded on grass
the blue of sky fixed in him;
he dreams of flashing through clear water,
casting his sheen and shadow
onto stones on the river bed.
Gills heaving now as he draws air
his lungs gulping for water.

Golden Carp

The pond in Habibah's garden
in Pataling Jaya is a tombola full
of golden carp, big and burley
they flick and flare under water.

I cross the stone bridge aware
of their ceaseless motion,
as if the lacquered gold of the sun
had fallen underfoot and caught

my eye and held it hostage to a shower
of light like coins of memory, like treasure.

Hare

Wakeful in early morning, night edging
out of the fields in the half-light the hare sits.

Only the twitch of his silky ears lets us know
he is here, alert, ready to kick off

and jinking run, unlike that crouching hare
caught and framed. This hare

is creating an illusion of motion
separating the thought from the deed.

a deception of making and remaking
himself at acrobatic speed, a dust-devil twisting

that way and this – a will-o'-the-wisp bowling along.
Light is brailling the landscape hooking him

in place, as he apes the grey dawn. He waits
for the fields to colour up and the empty air

to resume its constant hum. A living language
running on the land waiting for sunrise

to make its move. Waiting for its shadow
to rise up and break for the horizon.

The Sea Eagles Return to Lough Derg

Art is a civilised substitute for magic
Wyndham Lewis

Red tinged clouds stacked over the Lough,
the ruffled lake water bloody, I hold it in my eye
as I glide on thermals, telescoped below
are the rain glossed woods, the rocky bays,
small wind tossed islands. I have seen all this before
but not from above.

In another life I was the importunate poet, Aithirne;
they feared me, feared my ability, it was magical.
I could rouse both country and clans with well polished words.
King Eochaid laid on a royal spread, the boards bowed down
with hogs' heads, jugged hare, dressed pheasant
and butts of good strong wine.

Then I heard he held the best wine back.
Who better was he waiting for?
On leaving the place I named my tribute price. His eye.
The only one he possessed. He plucked it
from his face and threw the jellied mess after me,
his blood staining all the waters of the Lough.

I knew then he was more magical than me,
for his blood never dissolved, he renamed the Lough,
Dergheirc, Lake of the Bloody Eye. Sometimes I regret
those forfeit words so lightly tossed. The rest of my life
was not so charmed, I ended by being burned.
To this day the smell of singed feathers frightens me.

Now I have returned I inhabit the body of a white-tailed eagle,
I have no speech just a screeching noise that serves me well.
My cry drowns out the soft whistle of the wind,
rabbits quiver at my presence, fish in the lake
seek escape when my shadow clouds their sky
and I fly withershins above the water, counter to the sun.

Many Rooms, Many Doors

'The hundreth door may be the door to the heart.'
Theo Dorgan

My heart's valve is leaking.
They want to cut it loose.
It's moving inland in my body's

landscape, inscape even,
the way mist clears
from the bog in morning sunlight.

A slow uncovering of trees,
branches, leaves until a whole
bright wood is revealed.

Think, Imagine, Dream

'Poetry allows you to think, imagine, dream.'
Niall MacMonagle

Sometimes you have to dream first, dawn light
creeping over the edge of the fields,
sleeping horses float legless in early mist,
the neighbour's dog wolf-like in silhouette

watched carefully by the horses, some primal
memory alerting them, as we are alerted to the first dawn
of the winter solstice.
                Image ourselves back in time
                        to the wonder of filigreed light
on mica flecked stones

our hearts worn out with longing for the light;
our caves awash with line drawings
of our sheep and cows
and dogs and horses,
our children, our children.

Sticks dipped with mulberry dye, charcoal snatched
from the fire before it burns away. Fragments.

Then imagine,
your daughter   dream her into being,
imagine her red-gold head, hair burnished with sunlight
        her white, white skin, like fresh parchment
with nothing written yet

and her voice like the Linnet's song on the breeze.

Then think
what the world will bring, think of the wonder, the words,
the lurking sorrow. Think not of tomorrow, or nothing will happen
                                                today.

Today the black bog holds onto all its secrets,
its secrets are formed words from a tangle of sound

its unfathomable deep bogholes holding onto our ancestors bones,
the golden torc, the loving cup, the pin and clasp, the cloak long
rotted back to the weave of earth.

Lift your eyes to the light, let the roar of red on your eyelids
tell of its renewed power, let the clouds burst if they will.

Let the dog howl in the woods at night, let the horses whinny
their fright. Let the soft bog earth hold, let the light dance and dazzle,
let your golden headed white skinned daughter be,
to think, imagine, dream.

Frailty

I awake to a life constructed on light
and the fragile certainty of days.
A scrim of mist hovering in the far field
obscures the horses standing asleep.
Dreams cling opaque in this pewter dawn.
I reach towards the glossy fruit
on a tree, it seems to shrink
from me. Hungry I try again, can almost taste
its bleeding interior, sections of blood drop
luscious on my lips. The dangling fruit
changes to dancing Fuschia flowers
or the pink and orange berries of the spindle tree,
reminding me of dreams spun in the night.

The husk of a moth swaddled in silk
inside the folds of the curtains
dusted my foot as it fell. I untangled my limbs
from crisp linen as the urgency of day claims me.
Glossy eyed I no longer see the dream
as it sealed off and was swathed in mist
wind tattered clouds sailing by.
The horses shook themselves
awake, day took on its presence,
the sky soaking in constant blue.

Deposed

For seven years I was almost all hers,
despite an older brother and sister. I was the baby
cosseted and cuddled. Home from hospital and
almost dying, struggling for breath in my cosy crib.

A calling doctor brought me back into the world
with newfangled antibiotics.
We snuggled closer together
me sure of my foothold.

I was given into, my whims attended to, then shocked
when at my age of reason my slim mother's belly
ripened like a pod. I was all rage and unreason
when they tried to warn me my golden age was over.

I sat on the bottom stair, the others' punishment
step. Eventually through my mother's sobs and screams
I heard it, my worst fears,
the mewling cries of a newcomer.

I was outfaced, outnumbered. Twins, terrible twins.
I cried bitter tears. My gran and aunt exhausted
from hours in attendance came out from the magic
room, each bearing a caterwauling infant.

They showed me babies draped in swaddling blankets
with birth battered faces and murmured
platitudes about me being *Mammy's little helper.*
I viewed my deposers and understood my long reign was over.
The howling grew louder and I was struggling for breath again.

Patient's Notes

1

A beam of laser, like too-hot sunlight
burst your eye and the ophthalmologist placed it flat.
Sliced thin laid out in a dozen images.

2

Pinned and fanned on glass, the many eyes
of a peacock's tail passed in succession under
the microscope, life flashing by in slides.

3

See the snowy whiteness of a bassinet
your grandmother's plump hand dangling –
guarding you, the mythic white heifer.

4

Dim lights blink, a double vision of Dr.Coffey
and the twinned silver disk of her stethoscope advance.
Pneumonia. Both lungs. You're going under.

5

A milky whiteness seen from the corner of your eye,
a lace communion dress and you a lanky, one day princess.
Your sister dancing twirling steps to steal your thunder.

6

The pale blue yonder of your slivered iris, that speck in the left
corner of your cornea, dark rocks, an island in the Irish ocean,
covered and uncovered, washed in and out, making you seasick.

7

Galileo called his microscope the Little Eye,
it can create a world, but not the centre of the universe,
as our focus narrows to a pinprick.

8

We do the usual trick of squinting one eye
then the other, view the scene in parallax
as it jumps back and forth but will not steady.

9

You cannot take it in, as if the optic disc or blindspot
has taken over, your vision fills with that wooden box
balanced on your living room table.

10

Candled illumination in the darkened room
strips the naked eye, teaches you, a dim pupil
that it is your mother in the oaken cradle.

11

The ophthalmologist claims he has never seen the like,
the hysloid canal taken flat piece by flat piece
has become, to our surprise, a five-sided star.

12

It is the look of love, who knew it could show up like this
sliding in and out of focus, you cannot print it on the retina
it makes your freighted head dizzy, your socket sore.

13

Life goes on in tears and years each piling on another,
Some days your lids are heavy, as if weighted by silver pennies.

On Shellinghill Beach

'Oh the bells of hell go ting-a-ling-a-ling,
for you but not for me'.

from *The Dead Soldier*, Brendan Behan

Where I am is dank and dark, though I feel
the constant motion of the oyster-catcher and hear
the curlew and the wash of waves as they inch up
the mottled sand, that silvers out like dull coins in sunlight.
I have been buried here over thirty years,
here on Shilling Beach, where human kind betrayed me
and itself. My neighbours, for whatever God's sake.
I knew them, but didn't really, I wouldn't know their kind.

At night marram grass moans when the breeze blows low
over the strand. It was like a terrible creation, for six days
they tormented me, asking, asking, asking.
Entrenched, they had no answers, they flayed my flesh,
and on the seventh day rested a gun snug to my skull
and pulled the trigger. Ten poor souls dug into the dark
with me, my blighted children. Oh they remained in air,
but their spirits are harboured here.

When gulls call I feel the crumble of my white bones,
as the roiling sea sucks at me, I know its pull and tug
through the rising layers of sediment. All I did
was comfort a dying man. I didn't see his uniform.
He lay on the cold pavement amid cigarette butts
and dog turds and chip wrappers.
I wanted him to hear a human voice as his life ebbed,
to have a thread of sound to go down with:
Oh my God I am heartily sorry for having offended thee.

My ears got stopped with grains of sand,
but I believe they can still hear my voice calling
and calling like the curlew out over the years
and I sense somewhere at hand beside the constant, fluent
lapping of the tides, the answer of machinery and diggers
coming near. After that first death there Were Others.
The immensity of the capricious sea and froth of waves
on the shore are lacing and hitching themselves
like an eager bride in her veil.

Samoa – Into The Future

You jumped as one, not into your spirit world
of Pulotu, but crossed the line, changed time
propelled yourselves into a new dawning,
cast off the old and stepped through
time's portal, relummed into a fresh year.

At midnight, as one day ended the next in line
did not begin, it skipped a beat or like a stylus
on a vinyl record it leapt its groove and landed
one day later. This lost day is an artifice,
as in a leap year, it is a gap that thrusts

into the future. The missing day might have been
the day your were destined to die, or leave
your lover, abandon your child, fail your exams.
Abracadabra this is a reprieve like a lost
weekend that no-one ever mentions.

This is your brand new day. The sun rose
first on your South Pacific Island— greet it
with gratitude, tattooed it in your hearts.

* On December 29th 2011 Samoa skipped the 30th, to cross
the International dateline and went straight into the 31st.

JEAN O'BRIEN was born in Dublin where she now lives after an eight year sojourn in the Irish Midlands where she was Writer-in-Residence. She has four previous collections to her name; *The Shadow Keeper* (1997), *Dangerous Dresses* (2005), *Lovely Legs* (2009) and *Merman* (2012). Her Awards include the Arvon International Poetry Award, and the Fish International Poetry Award. Her work has been placed and highly commended in a number of other competitions including the Forward Prize. She holds an M. Phil in Creative Writing from Trinity College, Dublin and tutors in Creative Writing.